Writing Dissertations

Writing Dissertations

Alaine Hamilton

RIBA Publications

© Alaine Hamilton 1990

Published by
RIBA Publications Ltd
Finsbury Mission, Moreland Street, London EC1V 8BB

ISBN 0 947877 34 7

Other books in the Professional Communication series:
Writing Matters by Alaine Hamilton
Computers Count by Jaki Howes

Series editor: Alaine Hamilton

Book design by Penny Mills
Typeset by Goodfellow & Egan Ltd, Cambridge
Printed by Hollen Street Press, Slough, Berkshire

Acknowledgements

I am grateful to Stanley Cox, Nicholas Jones and Christopher Powell for help in
preparing this book.   A.H.

Contents

Preface

On holiday in Crete recently, I encountered a delightful lady who owned a jewellery shop in the town of Aghios Nikolaos. Sipping miniscule cups of coffee which had the temperature, consistency – and possibly the flavour – of boiling bitumen, we chatted about the relative merits of staying in or outside the resort. With devastating candour, my Cretan friend gave me her considered advice: 'I tell you that it is much better you stay in the town, in case you are boring in the country'.

I don't know (and I dared not ask) whether she had read *Writing Matters*, but I think I had better dedicate this companion book to my *rural* readers – and hope for the best.

Alaine Hamilton

Introduction

There are two main reasons for requiring students to write a dissertation as part of their diploma or degree examinations. The first is so that they can gain experience in how to conduct a systematic investigation into a particular subject area. The second reason is to give them an opportunity to investigate in some depth a topic within their area of study, and to demonstrate that they can present the results clearly and convincingly in good written English. Many tasks and commissions in professional practice require this kind of ability.

As well as personal diligence and application, the organisation, writing and presentation of a dissertation requires a methodical approach, an unbiased attitude, a clear view of the difference between fact and what is reported as 'fact', and the ability to marshall relevant information into a logical and coherent whole. It is something of a test of character as well as intellect, a stringent exercise from which, if all goes well, a student should emerge stronger as well as wiser.

Writing Dissertations
The first section of the book is about preparing for the task, choosing a subject and organising the necessary research. In Section 2 there is advice about the format and structure of dissertations, writing techniques and matters of style. Although much of the book applies equally to case studies and dissertations, there are some inherent differences which need considering, and these are discussed in Section 3. The fourth section reviews the techniques, formalities and conventions associated with the presentation of dissertations and other formal studies.

Writing Dissertations is a companion book to *Writing Matters*, in the Professional Communication series published by RIBA Publications, and will be found most useful if it is studied in that context.

Section 1

Preparation

1.1 Thinking ahead

You must be absolutely clear about the requirements and regulations governing the preparation, writing, presentation and submission of your dissertation. Read thoroughly all the information you have been given, and if there is anything you do not understand, ask for it to be explained.

The completed dissertation will have to be submitted by a prescribed date, and you will probably fail the task if you do not meet the deadline. Note the submission date in your diary and consider the practicalities of producing a major piece of work of this kind. Try to be realistic. Even if you get off to a flying start, there can be hiccoughs later: essential information may be unavailable, illustrations may have to be re-worked, substantial re-writing may be needed. As your research progresses, you might find yourself questioning the structure of the dissertation or even the validity of your line of approach. Be ready for the unexpected, and build into your timetable an adequate margin for contingencies.

1.2 Choosing a subject

If you are given a choice, pick a subject that *interests* you – one that will keep the adrenalin flowing and your motivation alive. At the same time, it must be one that is within your capabilities and circumstances and appropriate to the facilities you have available. It is usually best to avoid 'grand design' subjects that need a large input of time, money and people; consider a topic that is relatively small in scale but is intrinsically interesting and has potential for exploration and development. Your choice will also be influenced by the number of words prescribed for the dissertation.

Diploma or first degree dissertations are usually required to be between 5,000 and 10,000 words*. Do not stray over or under the limit by more than 150 words. Make regular word counts as the work

---

*To give you an idea of length, this book is about 11,000 words.

progresses so as to stay on target, and note the final number of words in brackets at the end. Be accurate: wily examiners have been known to check!

1.3 A literature search

Begin with a literature search to establish what published information exists about the subject of your study. This will provide you with a preliminary list of sources and will pinpoint key works.

It is wise to begin your search by consulting general reference works (see the Bibliography); these will direct you to more specialised information about your particular area of enquiry. Remember that your college or university librarian may be able to give you help and advice. All libraries have cataloguing systems, and it is sensible to learn how to use them, even if they seem rather complicated at first; they can save you a great deal of time in the long run. You may also suspect that you need more detailed information about the techniques associated with writing research studies. The Bibliography includes some useful titles.

1.4 Planning the work

Once you have put your thoughts in order and have chosen a topic, draft an outline of the study you propose. This should consist of a synopsis of contents, a framework and timescale for carrying out associated investigations, and a short bibliography. Then seek the advice of your tutor and other relevant staff. They will advise you whether you have made a suitable choice of subject and where and how to begin your researches.

Tutors are required to monitor the progress of dissertations and supervise their production. Agree with yours a programme for sending in drafts for comment and follow-up discussions. A tutor's continuing advice, constructive criticism and positive support can contribute enormously to the success of a dissertation. Be sure to keep your appointments with him or her, prepare for them properly, and make the most of them.

Be systematic. Consider the synopsis thoroughly and then write down the tasks that you need to carry out: letters to write, interviews to arrange, libraries to visit, books to buy or borrow, field-work and surveys to initiate, photographs to take. Make sure that you arrange them to form a logical programme of events, so that your information base grows steadily without gaps or repetition.

1.5 Keeping records

Be meticulous about keeping detailed records of what you have done, where you have been, whom you have met and what you have found out. Write up notes of interviews and investigations *immediately and fully*. Gather any supporting or background information at the time; if you put it off until later, the scene or situation may have changed. Carefully label and file all the items, make an index of them and keep it up to date. It is unwise to weed out apparently extraneous items as you go along: you may regret it later. Keep your options open until the time comes to sift and evaluate everything you have gathered.

1.6 *Writing Matters*

As noted in the Introduction, although this book is designed to be useful in its own right, it will be most effective if it is read in conjunction with *Writing Matters*, which recommends techniques for tackling all the main writing tasks that face architects in practice (correspondence, minuting, report writing etc), discusses knotty problems of grammar and syntax and suggests ways you can improve your writing. It is crucial to the success of your dissertation that your writing does not let you down. Buy or borrow a copy of *Writing Matters*, and then tackle the next Section.

Section 2

Writing the dissertation

2.1 Nature and scope

If you are tackling a dissertation for the first time, you may not be quite sure what kind of creature it is. Is it a research report, or some kind of learned disquisition, or a rather grand relation of the essay? The answer is that it is a bit of all three, but with a distinct flavour of its own.

A dissertation is like a report, in that it needs to be rigorously structured and must describe the rationale and methodology of the study and the research supporting it, and it is like a disquisition because it is an in-depth enquiry and often argues a case. However, in character it is probably more like an essay or a book.

As already noted, we are primarily concerned here with those dissertations that form part of diploma or first degree examinations; their length and the depth and scope of their enquiry is limited accordingly. The research involved is expected to be based on existing information, supported by a limited amount of empirical work.

A dissertation for a higher degree is a more substantial academic undertaking with a much longer timescale and of much greater depth and scope; it is expected to demonstrate a significant amount of original research and thinking and be a worthwhile contribution to the existing body of knowledge. However, whatever the scale of the work, the approach and methodology required remain the same.

Probably the best advice is to go and spend some time looking at the various dissertations associated with your subject which have been written in recent years. (Copies of dissertations are available in college and university libraries.) This will help you to get the 'feel' of this kind of study, and an idea of the scope, standard of scholarship and presentation that is required.

2.2 Formal structure

The format for a dissertation is rather like that for a report, but some items are also common to a book format. Fig 2.1 lists most of the items possible, but many of them will only be appropriate for a large scale or specialised study. Fig 2.2 is a contents list which is fairly representative for a first degree dissertation, but you should check this with your tutor, as your School or department may have its own recommendations or preferences. However, there are three principal elements common to all formal studies: the preliminary or front matter, the main text, and the end matter (which includes any appendices).

FIG 2.1
Structure and content of a formal study

1 Preliminary or front matter
Title page
Summary
Contents list
List of illustrations
Foreword by X
Preface
Acknowledgements
List of abbreviations
Any illustration relevant to whole work

2 Main text
Introduction
Chapters/Sections
Conclusions
Recommendations/Proposals

3 End matter
Endnotes
Appendices
Bibliographies
Glossary
Index

Front matter

TITLE PAGE
The first page of your study must show the title of the study and the degree or diploma with which it is associated, the name of the author, and the date. It is important to check the regulations for particular university or college requirements, in case administrative references also need to be included.

SUMMARY
It is often useful to include a summary (roughly a page in length) at the front of a report, so it might be appropriate to do the same for a case study. Ask your tutor about this.

CONTENTS LIST
Call the list 'Contents'. All the items in the study should be listed, including appendices, reference notes and bibliographies (see Fig 2.2).

FIG 2.2
A typical contents list for a short dissertation

CONTENTS	Page nos.
List of illustrations	ii
Preface	iii
Acknowledgements	iv
Introduction	1
Chapters	
1 Chapter title	3
2	8
3	17
4 etc	31
Conclusions	40
Recommendations/Proposals*	43
Notes to the text	46
Appendices	50
A1	
A2	
A3 etc	
Bibliographies	
B1	
B2 etc	
Glossary*	

* if appropriate

If there are numerous illustrations, list them separately immediately after the contents list. Head this list 'Illustrations', but note it in the contents list as 'List of ...'. Page numbering usually begins at the contents page, but if the preliminary pages are numerous (not likely with a study on a modest scale) they can have their own internal numbering system in Roman numerals; Arabic page numbering for the main text will then begin at the first page of the Introduction.

PREFACE

A Preface is optional. It usually contains introductory remarks by the author about his or her work. Unlike an Introduction, it is not *part* of the work. A Foreword (which consists of introductory remarks by someone else) is not usually appropriate in dissertations.

ACKNOWLEDGEMENTS

Here the author acknowledges any help or contribution to the study from others in the form of tangible information, oral advice or general support and encouragement. It is an author's personal statement of indebtedness and its tone should be appreciative, but not fulsome.

LIST OF ABBREVIATIONS

On rare occasions a list of abbreviations may be needed. The reader will find it most useful if it appears just before the main text.

End matter

ENDNOTES

Endnotes are a compilation of textual notes and references and can appear at the end of each chapter or section, or as one grand list at the end of the main text. The whys and wherefores of textual annotation are discussed in 4.3, with advice about the way to manage and present the notes. In the Contents, list them as 'Notes', or 'Notes to the text'.

APPENDICES

Although nothing of crucial relevance to the theme should be banished to an appendix, it is important not to clutter up the main text with extraneous material. However, to validate your study you may need to include detailed state-of-the-art information and examples, the text of codes, regulations and standards, extracts from relevant books and research reports, additional plans, drawings and photographs. All these items can be included as appendices and listed on the Contents page. The presentation of appendices is discussed in 4.2.

BIBLIOGRAPHY
A bibliography is a list of the sources, published and unpublished, which you have consulted in the course of preparing your study. It is an important part of a dissertation in that it indicates how thoroughly you have searched the literature, and supports and validates your work. Ways of compiling and presenting bibliographies are shown in 4.5.

GLOSSARY
A glossary is only needed in a dissertation if you are dealing with a subject which is difficult to describe without using specialist terminology. For example, you may have used computer techniques for analysing information and are unable to avoid using a certain amount of computer jargon. However, as a general principle, try to keep specialist terms to a minimum. A glossary is sometimes needed to clarify a technical report, and can be included at the front or back of the document. Only include one if it is really necessary and place it where it will be most convenient for the reader. An example of the style and presentation appropriate is included in 4.2.

INDEX
An index is indispensable in reference works, but is rarely appropriate in academic presentations, especially the short dissertations considered here. A full contents list, with page numbers, showing chapters or sections and their major sub-divisions, should be sufficient.

2.3 The main text: theme and organisation

Every example of discrete discourse must have a beginning, a middle and an end. Each of these primary divisions has its own function, and each should have its own internal structure. Flowing through the whole construct and binding together these divisions and sub-divisions is the theme, or subject of the study, which should develop and gather force until reaching its conclusion.

The beginning ('Introduction')
This part of the dissertation has to contain all the logistical information

about your work and is important in putting the study into perspective. It falls naturally into 'rationale' (why you chose this subject), 'methodology' (how you tackled the work), and 'theme' (the direction of your argument). Imagine that the examiner is asking questions which you have to answer. He might begin:

- Why have you chosen this particular subject?
- How did you approach the study?
- What actions did you take?
- Who helped or advised you?
- How have you organised the written and visual material?
- In what way are the appendices relevant?
- What kinds of bibliography are included and why?
- Where are notes and references to be found?
- Is there any background or scene-setting information that would help to put the subject into context?
- What is the scope of your study? Have you deliberately omitted some aspect?
- What is your theme or argument within the subject area?
- How are you going to progress it in the dissertation?
- Which are your major avenues of enquiry?

The middle ('Sections' or 'Chapters')
This consists of your selected major topics and can be thought of as a series of minor essays or chapters flowing logically and comfortably one to the next. They should preferably exhibit a similar treatment and structure, and each should be introduced and summed up and its relevance to the main theme explained. The sequence of the essays should relate to the power and relevance of each topic under review. If you begin with the weakest and progress through to the most cogent, you wind up your readers as you go along, preparing them for the conclusion. If your argument has been developed properly, this will seem inevitable. No conclusion should come as a surprise – if it does, your groundwork and theme development must be re-examined forthwith!

The end ('Conclusions', 'Recommendations', 'Proposals')
The function of the end part is to sum up, draw the threads of argument together and present your overall conclusions. You may go further and recommend actions prompted by your investigations, or forecast future trends, or pinpoint some area where research is needed.

2.4 Starting to write

Forget about beginning at the beginning and continuing until you get to the end. All you will do is ramble aimlessly on and on.

Using your synopsis as a basis, develop a simple structure under main headings. Break down each of these into topic headings. Then consider each topic in terms of a set of questions which need answering. Write them down. When you think you have finished writing the particular section, read the questions through and consider whether your answers are adequate. Then move on to the next section. It is a simple technique, but it works, and it also gets you into the habit of assessing what you have written as you go along.

Making connections

Each of the main topics or 'chapters' in the main text can be regarded as an essay in its own right with its own internal structure. The art is to make the various parts of the construct hang together, so that the whole theme moves smoothly onwards.

This is where the most skill is needed and where practice makes perfect. It is almost impossible to give rule-of-thumb advice; whole books have been written on the subject of theme development and progression. However, it may help to consider what is meant by 'writing in context', for this is what you should try to do.

Writing in context

The meaning of each clause or sentence depends upon the context in which it is formulated and expressed: that is, its intellectual validity depends in some sense upon what has gone before and what the reader expects will follow. The same concept holds good for para-graphs, which consist of sentences collected together to form a complete unit of thought. Think of paragraphs as beads of discrete thought, threaded together by a theme.

Does it hang together?

There is a good routine for testing the coherence of your prose. Read your work aloud, to yourself or to a friend. At the end of each sentence, pause. *There should be a question hanging in the air, and the next sentence should answer it.* Pause again at the end of that sentence, and wait for the next question. Repeat this test routine until you are reassured that your argument is hanging together – or until exhaustion sets in! Try it out on any 'serious' piece of writing, for example a leading article in *The Times*.

You may want to explore the matter further and analyse what it is about each unit of information that determines or influences its contextual relationship. It may be the way it has been constructed (syntax) or the words used (lexical choice), so that the reader is provided with 'clues'. The most effective writers tailor sentence construction to reflect the sense of what they wish to convey – in other words, grammatical relations are made to correspond with semantic connections. The late A J Ayer was a marvellous exponent of the art, and here is an example taken from *The Central Questions of Philosophy*[1], where he is considering the nature of perception:

> I may be in doubt as to what I perceive or what I feel, but I cannot be in any doubt as to their being *my* perceptions and *my* feelings. The suggestion that this headache might not be mine at all but somebody else's is quite nonsensical.

If you reduce what Ayer is saying to essentials, it is *I may doubt x, but I do not doubt y, and to suggest z is nonsense.* He uses the syntax to emphasise his sense of outrage.

For many of us, that degree of skill is a rather distant goal that can only be approached after much trial and error. In the meantime, there is at least one large caveat to bear in mind.

Be careful not to defeat the reader's expectations by leaving ends dangling, whether these are due to questions being left unanswered, or red herrings raised pointlessly, or simply through incomplete sentence construction. In other words, whatever you start, finish.

Reading aloud is an excellent way of exposing other undesirables such as unclear expression, awkward sentence construction, embarrassing ambiguities, and repetition. That leads us to the next matter to consider: an appropriate style of writing.

2.5 The style of dissertations

What kind of writing style is suitable for a dissertation? How formal should the language be, how personal or impersonal? A dissertation is serious and formal in character, and its tone and vocabulary should reflect this. However, it is not an impersonal exercise. On the contrary, it is *your* dissertation, on the subject of *your* choice, and it is up to you to describe and validate that choice. If the study ends with conclusions or recommendations, they are yours and yours alone. Therefore it is in order to refer to yourself as 'I' (although this does not mean, of course, that you should allow yourself to become chatty and anecdotal).

It is particularly important to avoid making value judgements (subjective estimates of quality), such as 'The interior design was unfortunate'. What you are saying is that *you think* the design was 'unfortunate', which simply means that you disliked it. In a serious academic work you are entitled to make observations, but you must always validate them. What you like or dislike is irrelevant, and may even put you on a collision course with the likes and dislikes of your examiner.

That said, on no account try to drain out of your writing every vestige of individuality or character. It is always difficult to find a style that suits the subject, that is accessible without being banal, fluent without being chatty, serious without being pedantic, and you will find no magic prescription for such a perfect artefact in this book – or anywhere else. A balanced and flexible style that can be adapted easily without any loss of personality is only achieved after much trial and error, and hard work. If you do succeed in achieving it, it will be an invaluable asset in your professional life. So persevere. In the meantime, it might be helpful to consider some writing styles that are definitely *un*suitable.

The Cold, the Dark, and the Ugly

The 'cold' is the remote third person style still often favoured for scientific and research reports. ('The liquid was observed to boil. It was concluded that . . .'.)

In the past, it was customary for this style of writing to be adopted to demonstrate the total impartiality of the reporter; unfortunately it came to be used whenever anyone wanted to write 'seriously' about anything. It is old-fashioned, tedious and lumpen.

The 'dark' is what is often referred to as the 'academic' style. Many writers fall into the trap of allowing their style to become inaccessible because the subject they are dealing with is difficult. All the more reason, you might think, for a clear and simple style when you are trying to throw light on a complex subject. Here is a relatively intelligible extract from the writings of Jacques Derrida[2]. As a thoroughly modern student of architecture, you will doubtless already have given Deconstruction an appropriate salute.

> When we investigate this "history" (but the word "history" belongs to this process of meaning) as the history of meaning, when we ask the "question of being" as a question of the "meaning of being" (Heidegger), are we not limiting the destruction of classical ontology to a sphere constituted by the reappropriation of the semantic plenitude of "to be", by the reactivation of lost origins, etc.?

That's murder, not English. Compare it with the clear, accessible prose of Stephen Hawking, one of the most brilliant theoretical physicists of all time. The reason his book, *A Brief History of Time*[3], is a bestseller is that he is able to express, clearly and simply, principles and propositions of the ultimate complexity which are far removed from the intellectual grasp of the average lay person. Hawking does not talk down to his readers: his gift is to make them feel that they have been allowed to share a little of his extraordinary insights, and to catch a glimpse of what it is like to be a genius.

Unfathomable academics like Derrida have always haunted our seats of learning, and probably always will. Fortunately, their influence is self-limiting because of the obscurity, not to say absurdity, of many of their utterances; in any case it is nothing new for language to be reduced by such people to the status of an 'intellectual' plaything.

Far more worrying, because it affects and infects communication at every level, is the insidious spread of bureaucratic jargon (the 'ugly'). The novelist Italo Calvino summed it up in *The Literature Machine*[4] when he said that we live in

> . . . an age of generic and abstract words, words good for all purposes, words good for not thinking and not saying anything, a plague of language that spreads from the public to the private sector . . .

George Orwell, dedicated campaigner against jargon, journalese and other forms of linguistic degeneracy, perceived this unpleasant phenomenon nearly fifty years ago. In his essay 'Politics and the English Language'[5] he described it as '. . . gumming together long strips of words which have already been set in order by somebody else, and making the results presentable by sheer humbug'. As an example he 'translated' this much-loved passage from the Bible into its modern bureaucratic equivalent:

> I returned, and saw under the sun, that the race is not to the swift, nor the battle to the strong, neither yet the bread to the wise, nor yet riches to men of understanding, nor yet favour to men of skill; but time and chance happeneth to them all.

> (*Ecclesiastes* 9:11)

Orwell's parody[6] is:

> Objective consideration of contemporary phenomena compels the conclusion that success or failure in competitive activities exhibits no tendency to be commensurate with innate capacity, but that a considerable element of the unpredictable must invariably be taken into account.

Jargon is not just a matter of using well-worn phrases (and remember that today's buzzwords are tomorrow's jargon); it is the outward expression of dull, unadventurous thinking, the linguistic equivalent of pre-packaged instant meals. Fight it!

2.6 Writing *matters*

However painstaking your research and colossal your brain power, all will be lost if you do not express yourself clearly, concisely and convincingly, and present your work pleasingly. The most common criticism made of reports and theses concern poor grammar, spelling and punctuation, and sloppy presentation. These distract and often infuriate examiners and, worse, tend to erode the validity of the study itself, negating all your hard work. Conversely, a study that is well written and attractively presented immediately creates a good impression.

In an extensive piece of formal work, careless errors are very noticeable. Do not dismiss them as minor deficiencies that are unworthy of your attention ('. . . after all, I am a *designer*, a *visual* person . . .' etc, etc). As well as not doing yourself justice now, you will be at a serious disadvantage in the real world of professional practice unless you recognise the importance of writing clear and effective English. (Read Sections 3 and 7 of *Writing Matters* in this context.)

It follows, then, that you must develop stringent procedures for assessing and checking your work. Do not be too proud (or diffident) to ask other people to help you: writing comes more easily to some than to others, and a frog, however well-intentioned, cannot expect to turn into a prince (or princess) overnight.

2.7 Assessing the result

It is important to assess the piece of work overall and to check that it is properly constructed and presented.

Checklist for assessing the study

1 Composition and theme progression
- Is the argument adequately developed?
- Is the study well structured? Have you tested it to see whether it hangs together?
- Does the argument progress smoothly to a conclusion?
- Does the conclusion relate to the aims of the study?
- Is the order of material logical, are groupings sensible?
- Is the style appropriate to the theme? Is it clear, economical?
- Is there anything that you ought to throw out because you are unsure about its source, veracity, relevance?

2 Writing ability
Read through your work, preferably aloud, to expose:
- awkward expressions, ambiguities
- repetition, generalisations
- value judgements, pointless anecdotes
- poor grammar
- spelling or typographical errors
- misplaced or missing punctuation

3 Organisation and presentation
- Does the page layout have eye appeal, is the text easy to read?
- Have you numbered the pages? If you have included page numbers in the contents list, do they match up?
- Are the detailed contents of the study consistent with the contents lists? Check the chapters or sections, appendices, illustrations – are they all there? Are titles consistent?
- Are the references consistent with the endnotes? Have you checked the numbering?
- Are there any discrepancies between the endnotes and the bibliography?
- Have you checked the accuracy of references? Quotations against sources? Captions?
- Have you included all the necessary acknowledgements?

References

[1] Ayer A J
      The Central Questions of Philosophy
      (first published by Weidenfeld & Nicholson, 1973)
      Penguin Books, 1976 (p 116)

[2] 'The Supplement of Copula' (a Derrida 'text') in Harari J V
Textual Strategies: Perspectives in Post-structuralist Criticism
Cornell U P, 1979 (p 117)

[3] Hawking S
A Brief History of Time
Bantam Press, 1988

[4] Calvino I
The Literature Machine
(Secker & Warburg, 1987)
quoted in *"My Native English"* (ed. Knight & Robinson)
Brynmill Press, 1988 (p 39)

[5] Orwell G
'Politics and the English Language'
(first published in 1946)
in *Collected Essays*, 2nd edition
Secker & Warburg, 1961

[6] *Op. cit.*

Case studies

3.1 Planning the work

A case study differs from a dissertation in that it is based principally upon personal observation of a real situation. In essence it is an empirical study of a specific case which provides the context for considering a selected theme. It requires a particularly systematic approach and a stringent analysis of evidence which leads to a concise set of conclusions.

Whereas a dissertation is most like a book or essay in character, a case study more closely resembles a report, and this is usually the most appropriate format to adopt. Although most of the advice given in this book applies to case studies as well as to dissertations, there are some important differences of emphasis.

Plan of work for a case study

1 Choose a subject
2 Decide a programme of action
3 Gather evidence
4 Check it with original sources
5 Test it
6 Check it against published work
7 Interpret it
8 Draw conclusions
9 Identify future trends*
10 And/or make proposals for further research*

*If appropriate.

The first priority with a case study is to establish a systematic methodology. When gathering evidence, always work to a plan or programme so that you know what to look for. Standing in the middle of a housing estate, say, and making a note of everything you see will result in a mass of unconnected items. Make sure that your records are properly identified, dated and filed systematically.

3.2 Evaluating information

The evaluation of evidence requires a rigorously impartial and analytical approach, and is often quite a test of character; it is always a temptation to 'bend' facts a little to make them conveniently fit your purposes and enhance your findings. Resist it: you will impress your examiners far more if you reject suspect evidence, saying why you are doing so.

You will need to evolve a suitable framework for evaluation. This is where it is useful to compare your work with other research done in the area so that you are not duplicating previous work or overlooking techniques and results that might help or affect your own enquiry. Arm yourself with a good working knowledge of the relevant published (and sometimes unpublished) information.

Interviews

Interviews are an important part of a case study, and you should be careful not to put words into the mouths of the people you interview. It is good practice to let them check through your records of meetings and sign them. Many people say things at interviews which they firmly deny a week later – be prepared!

3.3 Formal structure

The study should begin with an explanation of its rationale and methodology. Say why you have chosen this particular subject – it may be, for instance, that it is an interesting aspect of a project with which you are currently involved. Then describe fully the context of the study, since all the evidence you present will have to be understood within that context. It is often helpful to include area maps, photographs and site plans. You should also outline the scope of your work, explaining if and why certain features have been omitted.

Then explain how you decided to approach the study and what plan of action you adopted. Say where you went, whom you interviewed, what documentary evidence you obtained, what tests you made and so on. Only then present your evidence.

Evidence should be grouped logically and attractively and presented as the 'Findings' section of the study, supported by appropriate illustrations. The main text will end with 'Conclusions', and possibly 'Recommendations' or 'Proposals'. As we have noted, the report format can easily be modified to suit a case study. (Read Section 7 of *Writing Matters*.) It may also be appropriate to adopt a decimal numbering system.

Beware of relaxing your objective grip when you approach the usually welcome task of drawing conclusions and making recommendations. These must all be as tight and well-reasoned as the documentary part of the study – do not indulge in generalisations beyond the scope of your enquiry or in wishful thinking and rosy solutions.

End matter

You may wish to include appendices of extracts from research papers, sociological surveys, Government statistics, codes and regulations, fuller versions of meetings and interviews, or a more detailed exposition of your methods of analysis. An appendix containing additional visual material, particularly photographs, might also be useful. You should certainly include a concise bibliography of key works and recent research in your topic area.

3.4 Writing style

The style of a case study may be a little less formal than the style of a dissertation, since a case study more often discusses the actual than pursues the abstract. As a result, you may be tempted to adopt a 'journalistic' style of writing:

> 'I stood alone in the rearing shadow of Outsize House. Another sunset. Another tower block. Later, I talked with Darleen Bludgeon, 29, petite mother of eleven. She told me . . .'

Quite so. Now we have another category of writing style to toss into the dustbin of undesirables illustrated in 2.5:

> the Cold, the Dark, the Ugly – and the Unmeaningful.

Section 4

Presentation

The way you present the results of your investigations should reflect a thorough, systematic and consistent approach. The structure of the dissertation or case study should be taut and economical, its language clear and concise, and the finished document clean, well organised, easy to read and appropriately illustrated. The study should also handle well and be neatly bound, titled and referenced according to the regulations.

4.1 Using a wordprocessor

There are many advantages in using a wordprocessor for drafting a long piece of work: you will be able to key in and store material as the study proceeds, enter notes of interviews, record details of sources, keep an up to date list of action items, and rough-draft sections of the work ready for compiling and editing later. You may not own a wordprocessor yourself but it might be possible to arrange to have access to one for the duration of your study.

Keep an eye open for appropriate software. Packages are being developed which claim to help writers structure long research reports. Some of them provide readymade 'folders' and include various devices for setting out references, annotating the text and importing material from other files. One claims to be able to help the diffident writer to get under way by means of its 'brainstormer' feature, which is a kind of electronic bullying device which makes the victim write non-stop for a specified period just to get into the habit!

This kind of prop will not be needed by anyone who already has a clear idea of the structure and content of their study, and it may actually inhibit some writers.

4.2 Text preparation

It may be helpful to refer to Section 11 of *Writing Matters*, which deals with text presentation more generally.

It is assumed that the text will be typed on an electronic typewriter or wordprocessor. If you are not a competent typist yourself, find someone who is.

Use A4 white paper (vertical, not horizontal). The text should be surrounded by generous margins, approximately 40mm. The regulations may or may not specify whether single or double spacing should be used. A long double-spaced text on single-sided sheets seems (and is palpably) *very* long to the reader. Section and paragraphs breaks are not obvious, and the text often seems endless and monotonous. Therefore if you have to present the study double-spaced, try to break up the text by using relatively short paragraphs and by putting in paragraph headings.

On balance, single spacing gives the most pleasing and familiar result, but you must always follow the regulations. If it is available and permissible, one-and-a-half spacing might be a happy and attractive compromise.

If you are using a wordprocessor, you may be able to vary the size and/or density of the typeface or generate a different typeface, and you *will* be able to centre and justify displayed items. One way or another you should be able to produce a pleasing result. Remember that a lot depends on the printer you are using, so check what it can produce before you start. What you see on the screen is not necessarily what you will get on the printer.

Take special care to make the title page of your study attractive and inviting.

Headings

Use bold for headings, and establish a simple hierarchy of three or four main weightings. When you have completed a first draft, mark up in the margin the relevant weight of headings (A, B, C, D). This is an excellent way to check that structure and presentation are consistent. Fig 4.1 is a manuscript page where the headings have been marked up.

Italics (or underlining) should not be used for headings. Keep this for emphasis in the text, published titles, case law references, and unfamiliar Latin and other foreign words. Headings should not end with fullstops.

Quotations

It is usual to 'display' substantial quotations (of more than about 40 words), ie centre them five spaces in, single-spaced. No 'quotes' (single inverted commas) are needed. Smaller quotations can be run on in the

FIG 4.1
A hierarchy of headings

Writing Matters Sec 3 (Sep 88)   page 13

Ⓑ   3.7   Pitfalls to be avoided

Ⓒ Passive v. active

Avoid the passive voice - use the active. Compare <u>The
drawings were discovered by us to be inaccurate</u> with <u>We
discovered that the drawings were inaccurate</u>.

In the past the passive has traditionally been used in
scientific reporting to enhance the impression of impartial
observation (<u>the water was observed to boil</u> instead of <u>the
water was boiling</u>). Wherever possible use the active; the
passive is stodgy, unwieldy and creates a barrier between
writer and reader. It gives an impression of 'ivory tower'
pontification.

Use the passive <u>deliberately</u> for emphasis.

Ⓓ Examples

(a)   <u>I have lost my hat</u> [neutral statement].

(b)   <u>My hat has been found</u>! [marked statement].

Ⓒ Noun v. participle

Avoid <u>the (noun) of</u>; use the present participle. Compare <u>by
means of the use of</u> with <u>by using</u>; <u>by the modification of
the windows</u> with <u>by modifying the windows</u>, <u>for the selection
of a contractor</u> with <u>for selecting a contractor</u>.

text enclosed in 'single' quotes, unless they are of particular significance, when they should be displayed. Quotations within quotations should be enclosed within "double" quotes. Verse should also be displayed. There are several examples of quotations, displayed and otherwise, in 2.5.

If you are omitting part of the text you are quoting, or beginning in the middle of a sentence or not concluding one, you should indicate this by inserting a group of three dots (note: three only). If the omission is extensive, and you need to insert a word or words of your own to make the meaning clear, put it or them in square brackets. If the text quoted includes a word or phrase that seems dubious or even erroneous, the convention is to put *sic* beside it in square brackets. This represents a message to the reader: 'Even if this looks doubtful to you and me, this is the way it appears in the source quoted'.

EXAMPLE:
'However, it did . . . give [the employer] a contractual lean [*sic*] over the roofer . . .'

Illustrations

Illustrations included in the study should be relevant, not just cosmetic, and of good visual quality or execution (depending on whether they are maps, photographs, drawings, engravings, tables etc). If you have to photocopy and reduce any items, make sure they are still legible at reduced size. Plans should show a north point and drawn scale. It is acceptable to call them all 'Figures' (including photographs – to call them 'Plates' is very old-fashioned).

NUMBERING
Include Figures at suitable places in the study, with cross-references in the text, and number them according to the chapter or section in which they appear. Thus Section 3 figures will be numbered Fig 3.1, Fig 3.2 etc; Section 4 figures Fig 4.1, Fig 4.2, and so on. Remember that if you number figures consecutively throughout the study, any addition or omission will affect all the subsequent numbers and, if it happens at the last minute, this can be a disaster.

CAPTIONS
Captions should include full source information and acknowledgements where appropriate. Remember that some captions may be subject to copyright.

EXAMPLES:
> Fig 1.1 Whitehaven. View of estuary in 1939. Photograph by kind permission of British Rail.
>
> Fig 1.2 Southwark village. 'Disaster on market day'. Engraving by Samuel Poker 1835. British Library, London.
>
> Fig 1.3 London Docklands. Aerial view of City Airport, 1989. Photograph: Aerofilms.

If there are numerous illustrations, list them separately immediately after the main Contents list at the front of the dissertation.

Appendices

Each appendix should have its own title page and number, and its own internal page numbering. Its structure will depend on the nature of the material included, but try to keep the style of presentation consistent with the main text.

Glossary

Items should be arranged alphabetically. They look best if the explanation can begin on a new line. See the example below from *Computers Count* by Jaki Howes. Entries must be concise and accurate.

EXAMPLE:

ASCII
American Standard Code for Information Interchange. Has 256 unique identifiers for alphanumeric symbols.
Assembly language
A low level language which converts a programming language to machine code.
Back-up
Copies of software and data kept for security purposes.
BASIC
Beginners' All-purpose Symbolic Instruction Code. The most commonly used programming language for non-specialist applications.

4.3 Text annotation

You may wonder why it is necessary for the texts of dissertations to be spattered with notes. The answer is that academic work has to be demonstrably valid: statements have to be supported by evidence, sources have to be given, and references to published information have to be supplied in detail. Breaking off to include this important, but tangential, information interrupts the fluency of a writer's theme and the cogency of argument. For that reason, the device of textual annotation is adopted and is generally managed by means of footnotes or endnotes.

There are three main reasons for annotating the text of an academic presentation:

● to show sources of material referred to or quoted, ie to support and validate the basis of the study or argument;*
● to provide the reader with additional information which throws light on the context or historical perspective of events by, for instance, reference to other contemporary sources;†
● to convey the writer's own thinking or interpretation of events – a kind of 'aside' remark.‡

Examiners insist that textual annotation is properly organised and executed, so it is important to understand why it is necessary, and to get it right.

Footnotes
Footnotes are placed at the bottom of the page to which they relate, each with an appropriate symbol (asterisk*, dagger†, etc) or number which relates to its twin in the text (footnotes are included on this page as an example). In the past the convention was to rule off the text and site all notes at the bottom of the page, typing them single-spaced in manuscripts, or typesetting them in a very small typeface. This caused problems with page layouts, wasted expensive paper, and required complicated typesetting – and, in spite of all the effort, the result was often unattractive and difficult to read. (You will have seen old-fashioned textbooks where the footnotes take up twice as much room on the page as the text itself – for example, works by Shakespeare or Chaucer.)

---

*You will probably include in a bibliography some of the source references cited in the Notes.

†This might include reference to the economic or political climate at the time, buildings currently under construction, examples of contemporary art, and commentaries abstracted from the daily or technical press.

‡'Aside' footnotes are permissible provided they are relevant and contribute something to the argument. A dissertation need not be 'faceless', but be careful not to include too many comments – the reader might get tired of your face!

The tradition of adopting this kind of layout for learned books has persisted since mediaeval times, when monastic scholars spent whole lifetimes deciphering fragmented Classical texts, which they annotated with speculative comments of what the gaps (*lacunae*) might have contained. Nowadays, footnotes have largely been overtaken by the much simpler device of endnotes.

If you do decide to use footnotes for some good reason, keep them to a minimum. Remember that they are difficult to manage when your study is in draft, and could cause you nerve-wracking problems with page layouts if you decide at the eleventh hour to transpose paragraphs or include additional material.

Endnotes

Endnotes are a compilation of all textual notes and can appear at the end of each chapter or section to which they relate, or in one grand list at the end of the main text. This device is easy to manage and is appropriate for dissertations on a relatively modest scale. Reference numbers are typed into the line of text in brackets, or superscribed, and each number refers to an endnote. Continuous numbering through the whole text is very unwise for the reasons already explained in relation to illustrations.

Endnotes have been used for the literary references in Section 2 as an example, and Fig 4.2 shows alternative ways of including the related numbers in the text.

FIG 4.2
Endnote numbers

```
        The novelist Italo Calvino summed it up in
        The Literature Machine(4) when he said ...

        The novelist Italo Calvino summed it up in
        The Literature Machine(4) when he said ...


        The novelist Italo Calvino summed it up in

        The Literature Machine[4] when he said ...


        The novelist Italo Calvino summed it up in

        The Literature Machine4 when he said ...
```

4.4 Source references

All sources referred to, published or unpublished, should be fully documented the first time they are given and, as discussed above, included in a list of endnotes.

The purpose of including references is to make sure that the necessary information is given to enable the reader to identify and retrieve items from a library, collection or archive. As with endnotes, this is something that you must get right in your study. References must be accurate and their presentation must be logical and consistent.

The two categories of book reference most commonly used are the full reference and the short. A full reference should always be supplied the first time a work is mentioned; thereafter a short reference can be used.

A full reference should include:

> Author, surname first
> Full title of work
> Editor, translator or compiler
> Series in which book appears
> Edition, if not the first, and name of reviser
> Number of volumes (if more than one)
> Place of publication (if not London)
> Name of publisher
> Year of publication
> Volume reference and
> page reference

EXAMPLE:
Jones, A Q
Plants, Pots and Patios
3rd ed. (rev. Greenfinger)
Mulberry Books, 1987
2: pp 62–67

A short reference only has to contain enough information for the reader to identify a reference that has already been given in full.

EXAMPLE:
Jones, *Plants, Pots* etc
pp 132–133

In the case of articles in periodicals, a full reference should include:

Author
Title of article
Title of periodical
Volume number and part
Date of publication
Page reference of article, then particular reference

EXAMPLE:
Proust, R P
'Stones and glass roofs'
Architectural Review 171, Pt 3
July 1987, pp 58–62 (59)

The short version would be:

EXAMPLE:
Proust, 'Stones and glass roofs'
p 59

If space permits, set out references on several lines, as in the examples above. The convention is to put the titles of publications into italics (or underline them), and the titles of articles into single quotes. Numbers (of editions, volumes, pages etc) are written in Arabic numerals, although volume numbers are sometimes set in Roman. You will see from the examples that the amount of punctuation can vary according to the way the item has been laid out. References look less cluttered if you leave out superfluous commas, but always include them if they are needed for clarity.

4.5 Bibliographies

A bibliography is an important part of a dissertation in that it indicates how thoroughly you have searched the literature, and supports and validates your study.

It is sometimes appropriate to include a selected bibliography of seminal or specialist sources. A general bibliography of related as well as representative material may also be appropriate.

When you have decided how to group the source material, arrange each list in alphabetical order according to the surname of the author. Use a full reference for each title. Any unpublished material included should be listed separately – in a separate bibliography, if it is extensive.

Bibliographical entries

Each should be a full reference to the work in question. You may already have cited it fully in a list of endnotes; the bibliographical entry will be the same, minus any page references.

EXAMPLES:
Published books and articles

Jones, A Q
Plants, Pots and Patios
3rd ed. (rev. Greenfinger)
London: Mulberry Books, 1987

Proust, R P
'Stones and Glass Roofs'
Architectural Review 171, Pt 3
July 1987

Unpublished material

Outsize House, Hackney, London
Ms logbook kept by Bludgeon, D
January – October 1988

Windbag, C J
'Warts and Boils in Twentieth Century Urban Design'
PhD thesis: King's College London, 1982

4.6 Latin words and phrases

Once again, we are back in the Middle Ages when Latin was the only written language and all the scholarship that existed took place in the monasteries. A knowledge of Latin became the mark of an educated person and was required for entry into the learned professions. Even today, the medical and legal professions like to preserve their respective mystiques by liberal sprinklings of Latin words (often of a bastardised variety that would make Cicero shudder) in prescriptions and legal documents.

Latin words and abbreviations are commonly used in referencing systems, and it is as well to know what they mean and how they are used. Here is an explanation of the ones you are most likely to encounter.

&, &c.

& is the sign that stands for *and* (or *et* in Latin). It is called an *ampersand*, which is a corruption of 'and per se and'. The sign evolved from the scribbled Latin *et*, as you can see (&), and may be used in bibliographical references where there are two joint authors, eg Proust & Jones. Where there are more, it is usual to write Proust, Jones and Windbag etc. The ampersand can also be used where it is part of a company name (eg Rushe & Roulette). Otherwise, & should be spelt out. Similarly, &c. should become *etc.* except where it appears in an original which is being quoted. It is short for *et cetera*, meaning *and the rest, and so on*.

c., ca

c. or ca (short for *circa*) means *about* or *approximately*. It is commonly used with dates, eg 'the house was built *c.* 1790'. The convention is to put it into italics.

eg, ie

eg (short for *exempli gratia*) means *for example*; ie means *that is* (Latin *id est*). With both, make sure that you are consistent about using or omitting punctuation, 'eg like this', or 'e.g., like this'.

et al.

et al. means *and the others (alii* meaning *other people*, and *alia* meaning *other things*). It is used in short references to works which have more than two authors, eg 'Proust et al.', although the rule is that the first mention of a multi-author work should give them all.

et seq., f and ff

et seq. (short for *et sequens*) means *and following*. It is used in page references, eg pp 75 *et seq.* It is an imprecise reference, although its use is widespread. A slightly better alternative is to use f and ff (short for *following*) where 'pp 23f' means p 23 and the next page, and 'pp 23ff' means page 23 and (any number of) following pages. In your own work, go to the trouble of specifying the actual page numbers in question, eg 'pp 23–27'. This is not only more helpful to the reader, but more elegant.

ibid., op. cit., loc. cit.

ibid. (short for the adverb *ibidem*) means *in the same book, chapter, passage* etc. and is often seen in footnotes. It is convenient in that it spares the author the trouble of repeating a reference already given. *Op. cit.* (short for *opere citato*) meaning *in the work already quoted*, is used in the same way, and so is loc. cit. (*loco citato*), meaning *in the passage already quoted*).

A word of warning about these 'convenience' items. In some quarters they are regarded as evidence of laziness on the part of the writer, so it may be better to play safe and include a short reference instead. On the other hand, it can reasonably be argued that where numerous references to the same work appear closely together, it looks pretty silly to keep repeating them. You must use your judgement.

v.

v. is short for *versus*, meaning *against*, and is used in references to legal cases, eg *Crumb v. Jellybean 1896*.

Avoid using Latin where there is a perfectly good English alternative: you risk appearing stuffy and pedantic – and your reader may not understand what you mean. If you have to use legal terms such as *contra proferentem, quantum meruit*, put them into italics, but do not italicise Latinisms that have long since been adopted into English, such as vice versa, status quo, per se, non sequitur, unless there is a danger of confusion with English words (eg *vice* and 'vice'). Similarly, avoid using Roman numerals for sub-lists. They look old-fashioned, and nowadays it is more usual to write (a), (b), (c) etc, or to use Arabic numerals or bullet points.

4.7 At the eleventh hour

Read the regulations again to make sure that you have complied with the requirements for binding and the number of bound copies to be supplied. Remember to keep an extra copy or copies for your own use, as submitted copies become the property of the college or university. To recap, the title page must show the name of the author, the title of the dissertation, the degree with which it is associated, the date, and any administrative references required. The author's name and the title of the study should also be printed on the spine, together with the appropriate reference number.

You may have to submit an abstract, usually of about 500 words, and there may be guidance about the way this should be presented. An abstract is simply a summary of the theme and conclusions of your study for at-a-glance reference.

Last minute checklist

- Does the finished work look attractive?
- Is it clean, easy to handle?
- Has everything been included in all the copies?
- Have you complied with all the regulations for submission?

Now all you have to do is watch and pray!

Bibliography

RIBA Book List
Published every year, and compiled by the RIBA's Professional Literature Committee. This is an excellent general guide and should be a first point of reference for architectural books. All the books listed may be consulted in the British Architectural Library, which is one of the finest in the world, and borrowed by RIBA Members and Students. The *Book List* directs readers to other information sources, dictionaries and encyclopaedias, bibliographies, and new and established titles on all aspects of the history and practice of architecture.

The AJ Information Guide
Published annually as a supplement to the *Architect's Journal*. A useful companion to the *RIBA Book List*.

Architectural Periodicals Index (API)
Compiled by the British Architectural Library. A comprehensive index of the contents of some 300 journals worldwide. The Index is available on-line.

Berry, Ralph
How to write a research paper
2nd edition
Oxford: Pergamon Press, 1986

Butcher, Judith
Copy-editing: the Cambridge handbook
2nd revised edition
Cambridge University Press, 1983

Gowers, Sir Ernest
The complete plain words
(rev. Greenbaum & Whitcut)
Penguin Books, 1987

Hamilton, Alaine
Writing matters
Professional Communication series
RIBA Publications, 1989

Hoffman, Ann
Research for writers
3rd edition
A & C Black, 1986

Howes, Jaki
Computers count
Professional Communication series
RIBA Publications, 1989

Index

Index

Margins *see Text preparation*
Methodology 2.3

op. cit. 4.6
Orwell G, 2.5

Page layout *see Text preparation*
Photographs *see Appendix*
Preface 2.2
Preliminaries 2.2
Printers *see Wordprocessing*
Punctuation 2.6

Quotation marks *see Text preparation*
Quotations *see Text preparation*

Recommendations 2.3
Records, index of 1.6
References
    administrative 2.2, 4.7
    full 4.4
    short 4.4
    to articles 4.4
    to periodicals 4.4
    use of Latin words 4.6
Regulations 1.2, 4.7
Research 1.4

Software *see Computer*
Source references *see References*

Spacing, double or single *see Text preparation*
Spelling 2.6
Style *see Writing*
    of dissertations 2.5
    of case studies 3.4
Subject, choice of 1.3
Superscripts *see Text annotation*
Synopsis 1.5
Syntax 1.7, 2.4

Text
    annotation 4.3
    organisation 2.3
    preparation 2.2, 4.2
Theme
    progression 2.3, 2.7
    coherence 2.4
Title page 2.2, 4.7
Tutor, advice of 1.5

Unpublished sources *see Bibliography*

Verse, display of *see Text preparation*
v. and *versus* 4.6

Word count 1.3
Wordprocessing 4.1, 4.2
Writing
    competence 1.7, 2.7
    styles 2.5, 3.4